play guitar with...

rodrigo y gabriela

diablo rojo 12

hanuman 16

the russian messenger 27

santo domingo 36

the soundmaker 45

tamacun 55

Published by
Wise Publications
14-15 Berners Street, London W1T 3LJ, UK.

Exclusive Distributors:
Music Sales Limited
Distribution Centre, Newmarket Road,
Bury St Edmunds, Suffolk IP33 3YB, UK.
Music Sales Pty Limited
4th floor, Lisgar House, 30-32 Carrington Street,
Sydney, NSW 2000, Australia.

Order No. AM1009987
ISBN 978-1-78305-835-8
This book © Copyright 2015 Wise Publications,
a division of Music Sales Limited.

Edited by Adrian Hopkins.
Cover designed by Tim Field.
Music engraved by Paul Ewers Music Design.
Guitars recorded by Arthur Dick.
All audio mastered and mixed by Jonas Persson.
Printed in the EU.

www.musicsales.com

WISE PUBLICATIONS
part of The Music Sales Group
**London / New York / Paris / Sydney / Copenhagen /
Berlin / Madrid / Hong Kong / Tokyo**

guitar tablature explained

Guitar music can be explained in three different ways: on a musical stave, in tablature, and in rhythm slashes.

RHYTHM SLASHES: are written above the stave. Strum chords in the rhythm indicated. Round noteheads indicate single notes.

THE MUSICAL STAVE: shows pitches and rhythms and is divided by lines into bars. Pitches are named after the first seven letters of the alphabet.

TABLATURE: graphically represents the guitar fingerboard. Each horizontal line represents a string, and each number represents a fret.

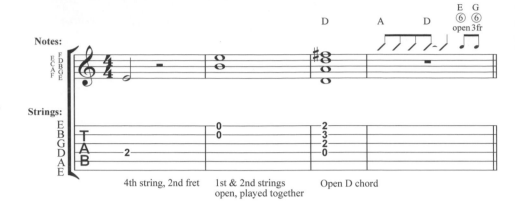

4th string, 2nd fret   1st & 2nd strings open, played together   Open D chord

definitions for special guitar notation

SEMI-TONE BEND: Strike the note and bend up a semi-tone (½ step).

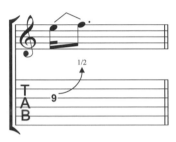

WHOLE-TONE BEND: Strike the note and bend up a whole-tone (full step).

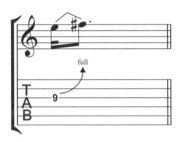

GRACE NOTE BEND: Strike the note and bend as indicated. Play the first note as quickly as possible.

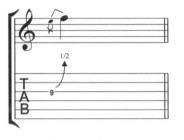

QUARTER-TONE BEND: Strike the note and bend up a ¼ step

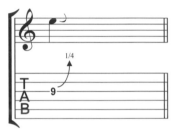

BEND & RELEASE: Strike the note and bend up as indicated, then release back to the original note.

COMPOUND BEND & RELEASE: Strike the note and bend up and down in the rhythm indicated.

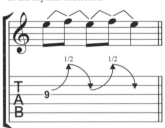

PRE-BEND: Bend the note as indicated, then strike it.

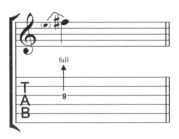

PRE-BEND & RELEASE: Bend the note as indicated. Strike it and release the note back to the original pitch.

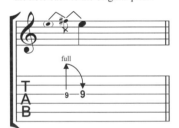

HAMMER-ON: Strike the first note with one finger, then sound the second note (on the same string) with another finger by fretting it without picking.

PULL-OFF: Place both fingers on the note to be sounded, strike the first note and without picking, pull the finger off to sound the second note.

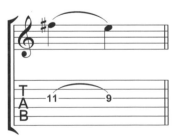

LEGATO SLIDE (GLISS): Strike the first note and then slide the same fret-hand finger up or down to the second note. The second note is not struck.

MUFFLED STRINGS: A percussive sound is produced by laying the first hand across the string(s) without depressing, and striking them with the pick hand.

NATURAL HARMONIC: Strike the note while the fret-hand lightly touches the string directly over the fret indicated.

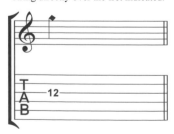

PICK SCRAPE: The edge of the pick is rubbed down (or up) the string, producing a scratchy sound.

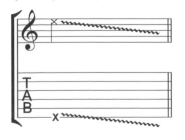

PALM MUTING: The note is partially muted by the pick hand lightly touching the string(s) just before the bridge.

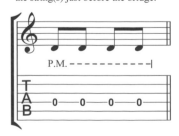

SHIFT SLIDE (GLISS & RESTRIKE) Same as legato slide, except the second note is struck.

special percussion techniques

The following notation is used in this book to try and illustrate the unique percussive playing techniques used by Rodrigo Y Gabriela. These are particularly relevant to the rhythmic accompanying parts performed by Gabriela. Experiment with these techniques, and study the original recordings, to emulate her sound:

Percussive hit, either on the bridge (for a low sound), or on the fretboard (for a sharper sound). This is performed with varying degrees of muting with the fretting hand to create different effects.

Chord hit. Some accented chords are given extra attack by a flick of the index finger, creating a very powerful sound.

Muted stroke. The strings are muffled by the fretting hand, and then a played to produce a percussive sound with upstrokes and downstrokes of either the fingers or thumb.

Hit to body of the guitar with knuckles or fingers (either of the fretting hand for accents or both hands for more extended percussive sections).

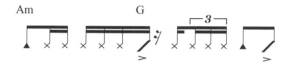

This is a typical example of the parts that Gabriela plays, combining hits with accented chords and muted notes. Different combinations of upstrokes and downstrokes using the index and middles fingers, and thumb are used to execute these kind of figures. Typically, alternating upstrokes and downstrokes are used. Triplet figures are played by a downstroke with the fingers followed by a further downstroke with the thumb and lastly an upstroke with the thumb.

Percussive sections: extended figures like this are performed by either drumming on the body of the guitar with the fingers and knuckles (Gabriela) or drumming below the soundhole with the fingers (Rodrigo).

additional musical definitions

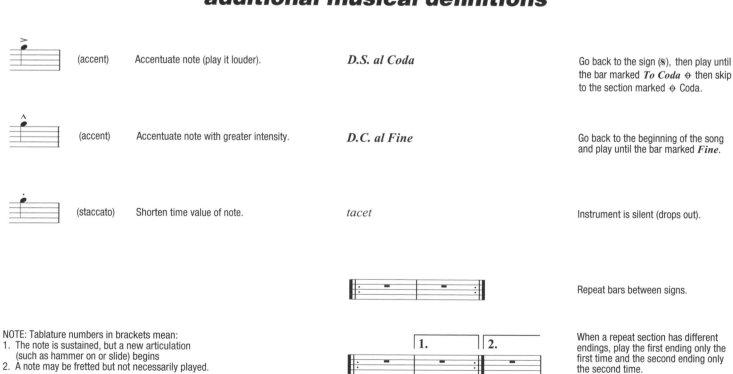

(accent) — Accentuate note (play it louder).

(accent) — Accentuate note with greater intensity.

(staccato) — Shorten time value of note.

D.S. al Coda — Go back to the sign (𝄋), then play until the bar marked **To Coda** ⊕ then skip to the section marked ⊕ Coda.

D.C. al Fine — Go back to the beginning of the song and play until the bar marked **Fine**.

tacet — Instrument is silent (drops out).

Repeat bars between signs.

When a repeat section has different endings, play the first ending only the first time and the second ending only the second time.

NOTE: Tablature numbers in brackets mean:
1. The note is sustained, but a new articulation (such as hammer on or slide) begins
2. A note may be fretted but not necessarily played.

diablo rojo

Music by Rodrigo Sanchez & Gabriela Quintero

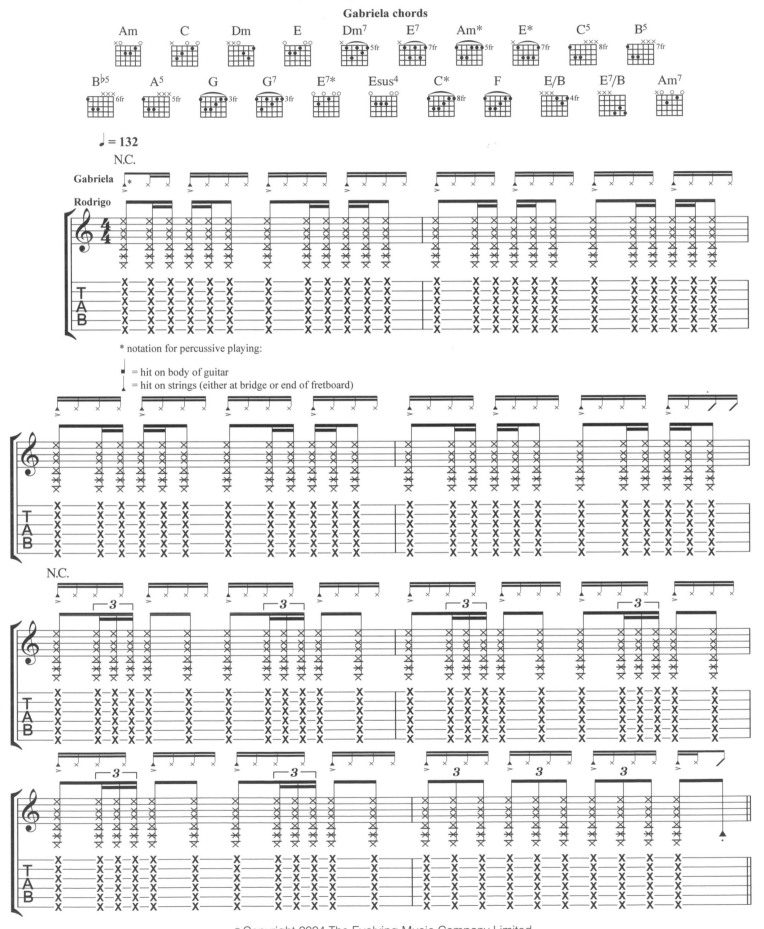

* notation for percussive playing:

= hit on body of guitar

= hit on strings (either at bridge or end of fretboard)

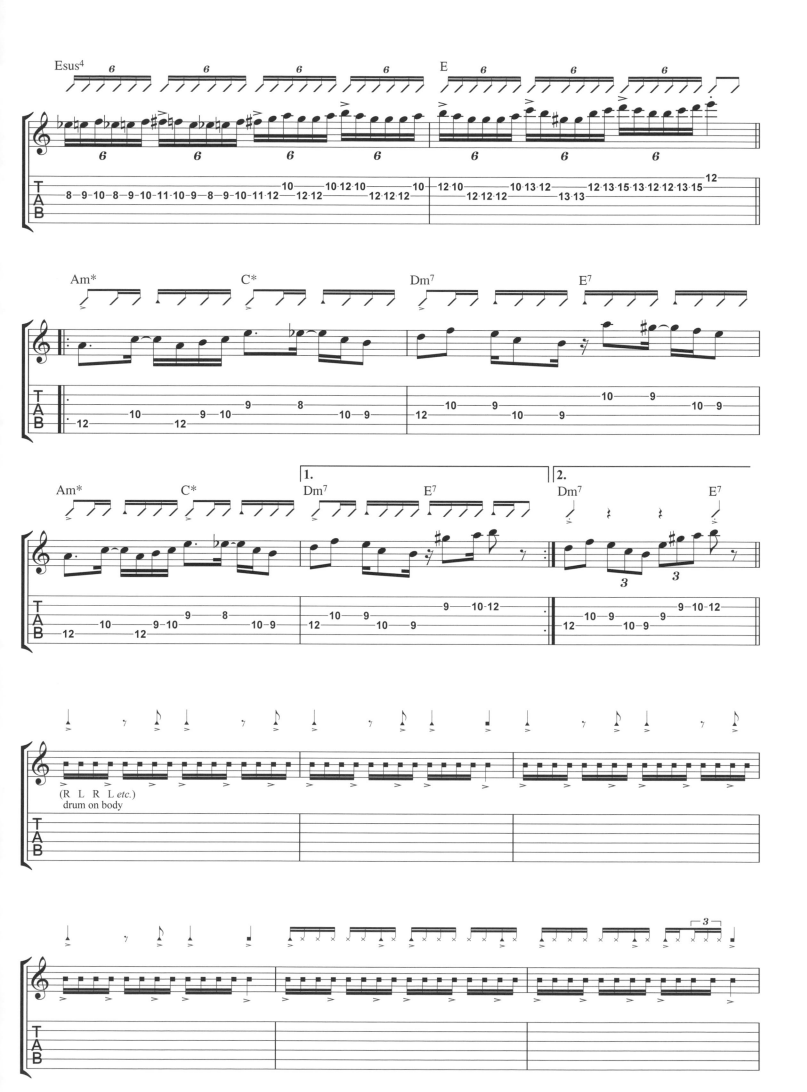

7

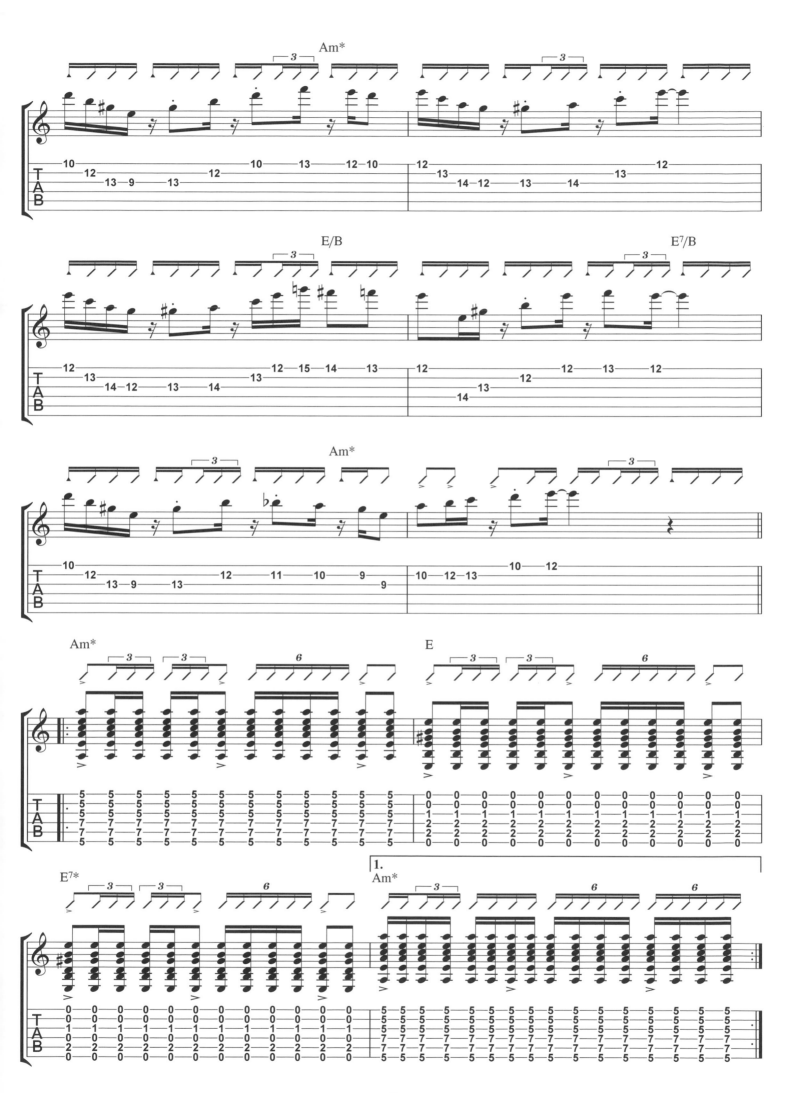

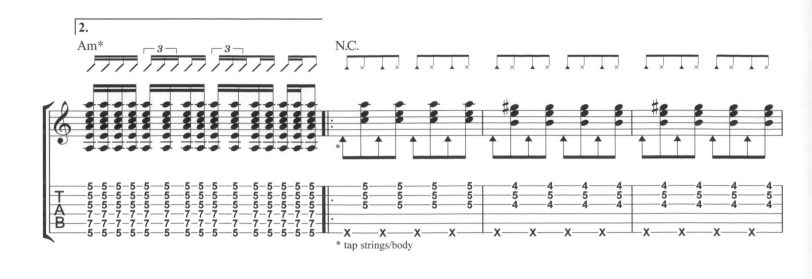

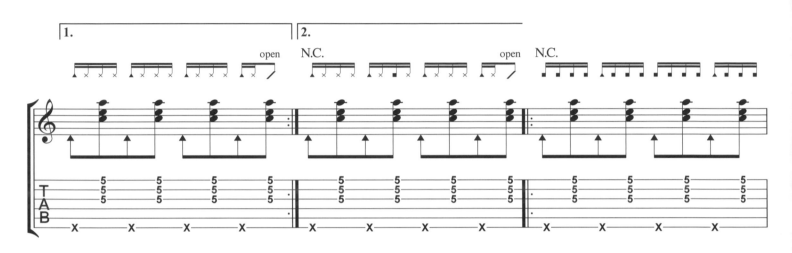

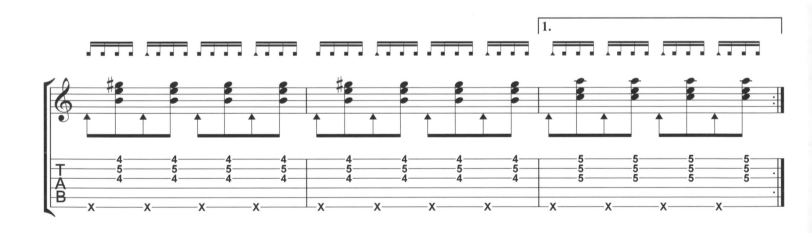

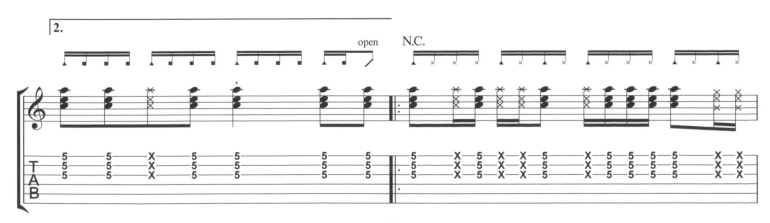

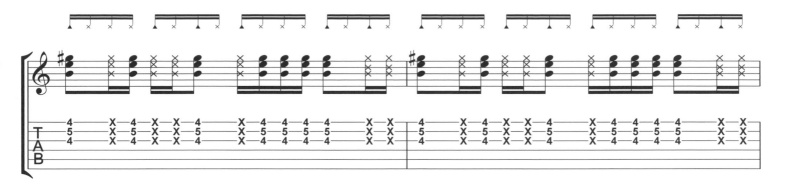

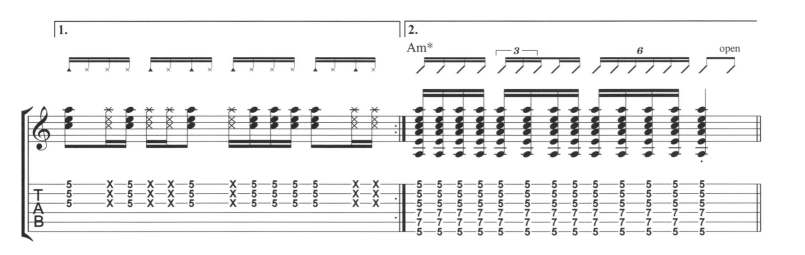

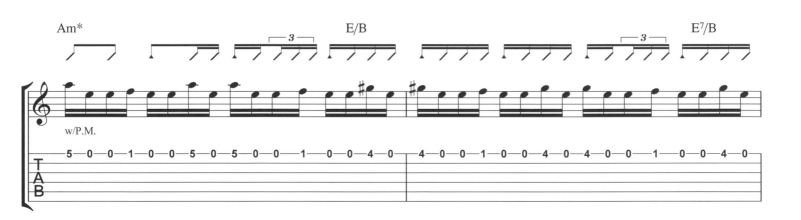

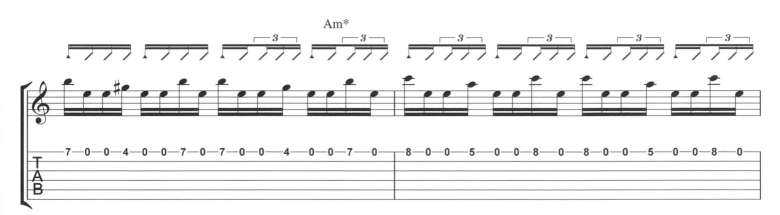

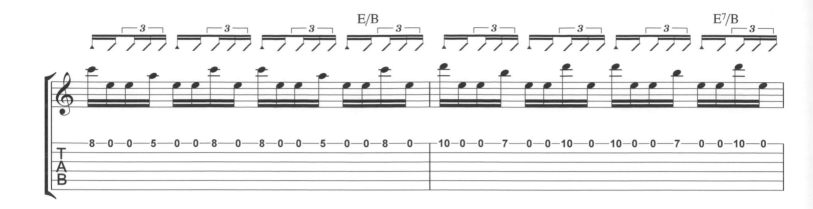

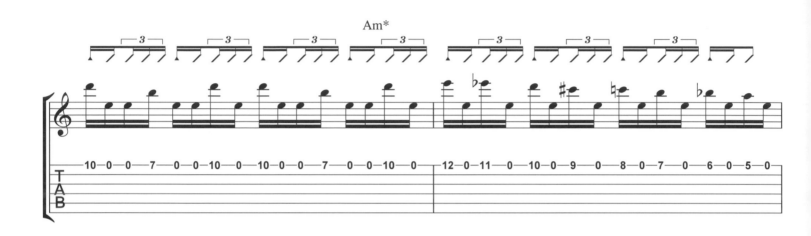

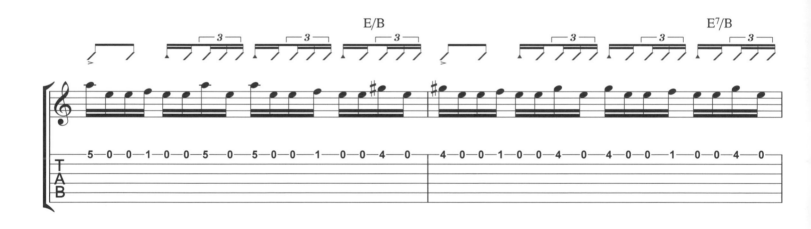

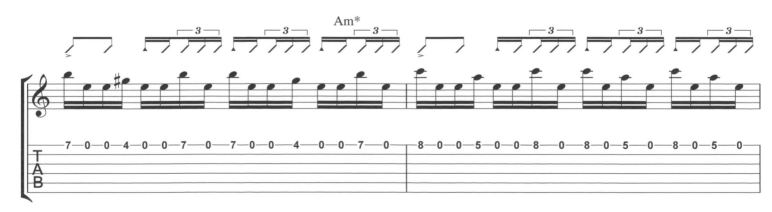

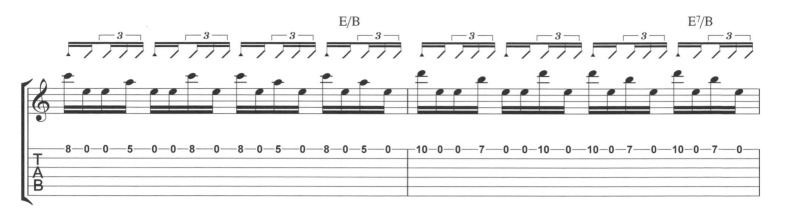

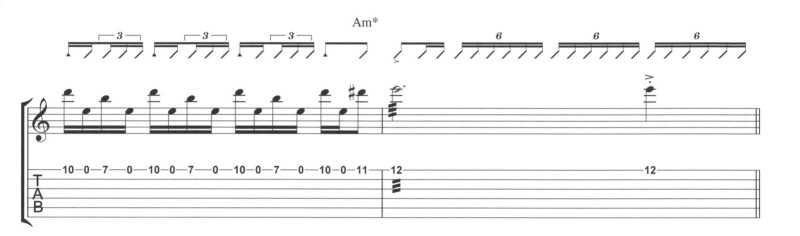

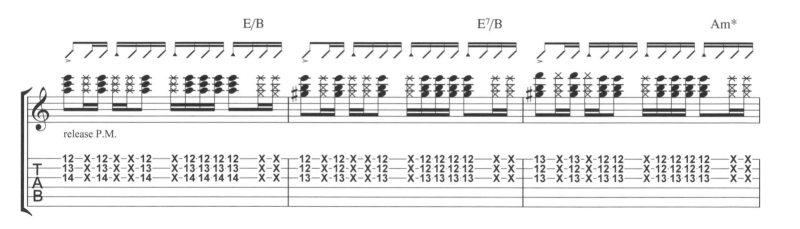

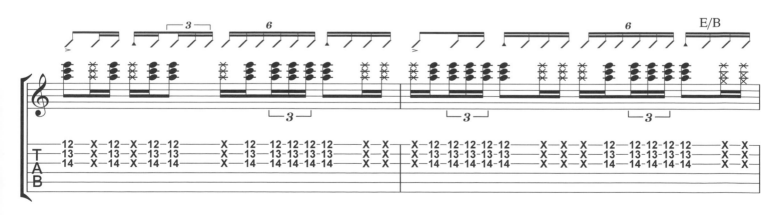

13

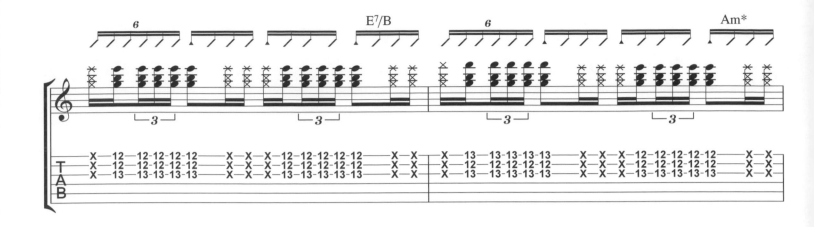

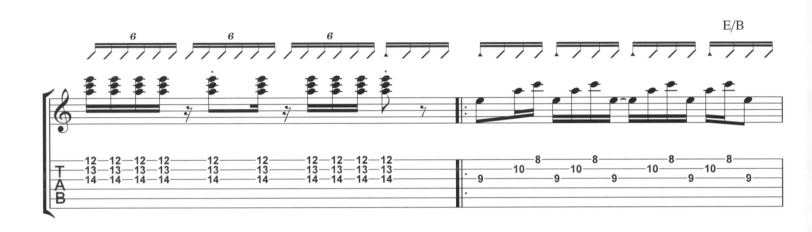

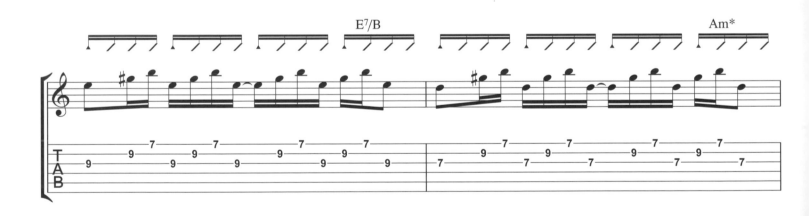

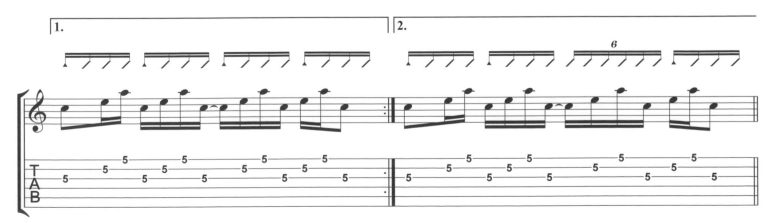

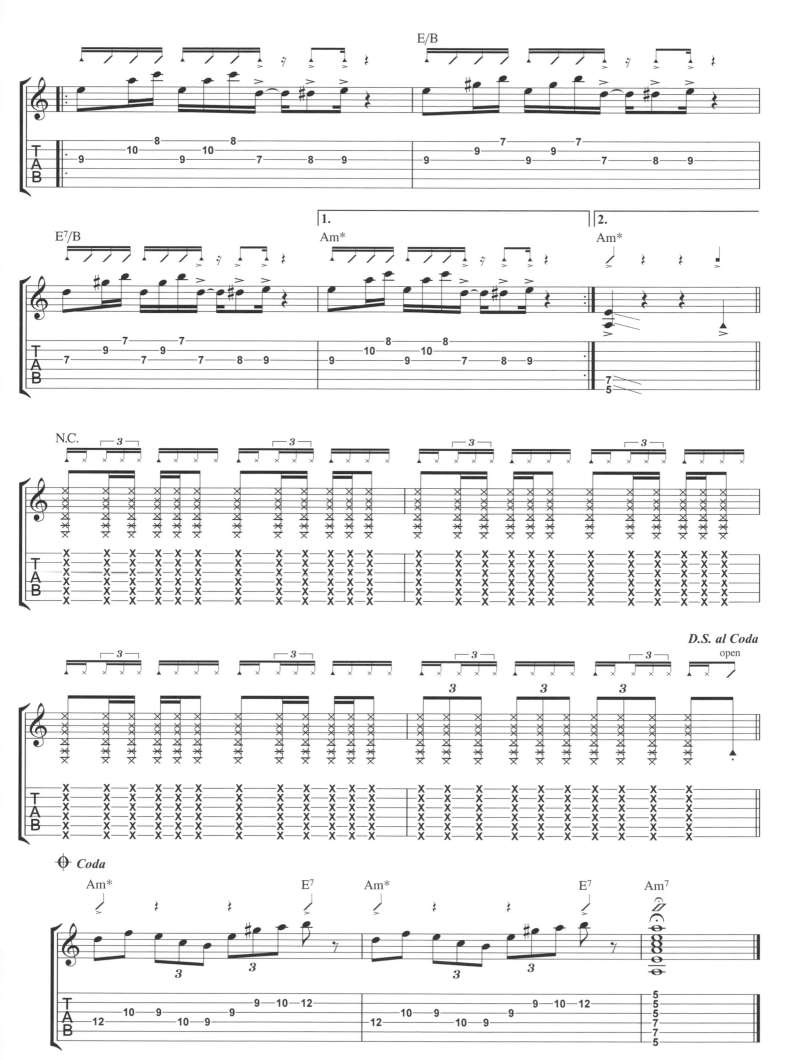

15

hanuman

Music by Rodrigo Sanchez & Gabriela Quintero

16

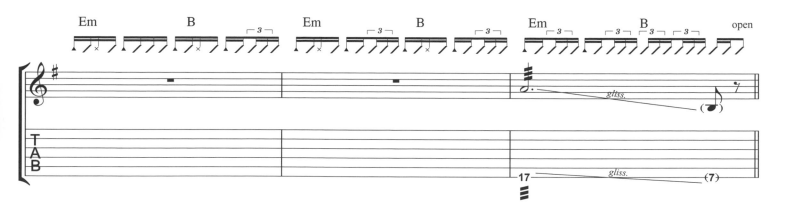

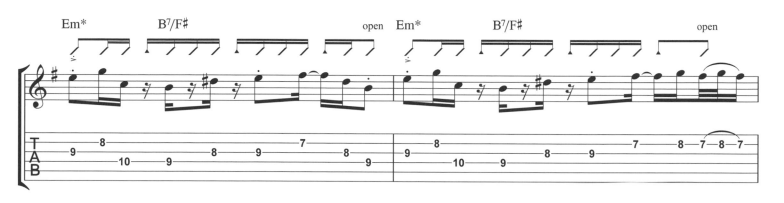

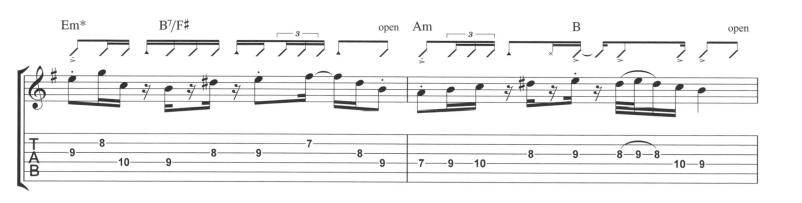

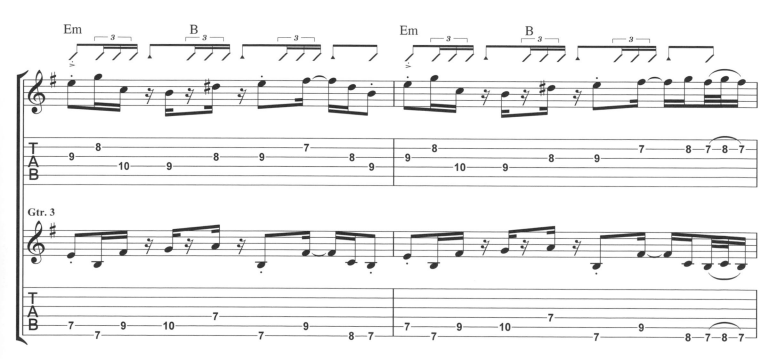

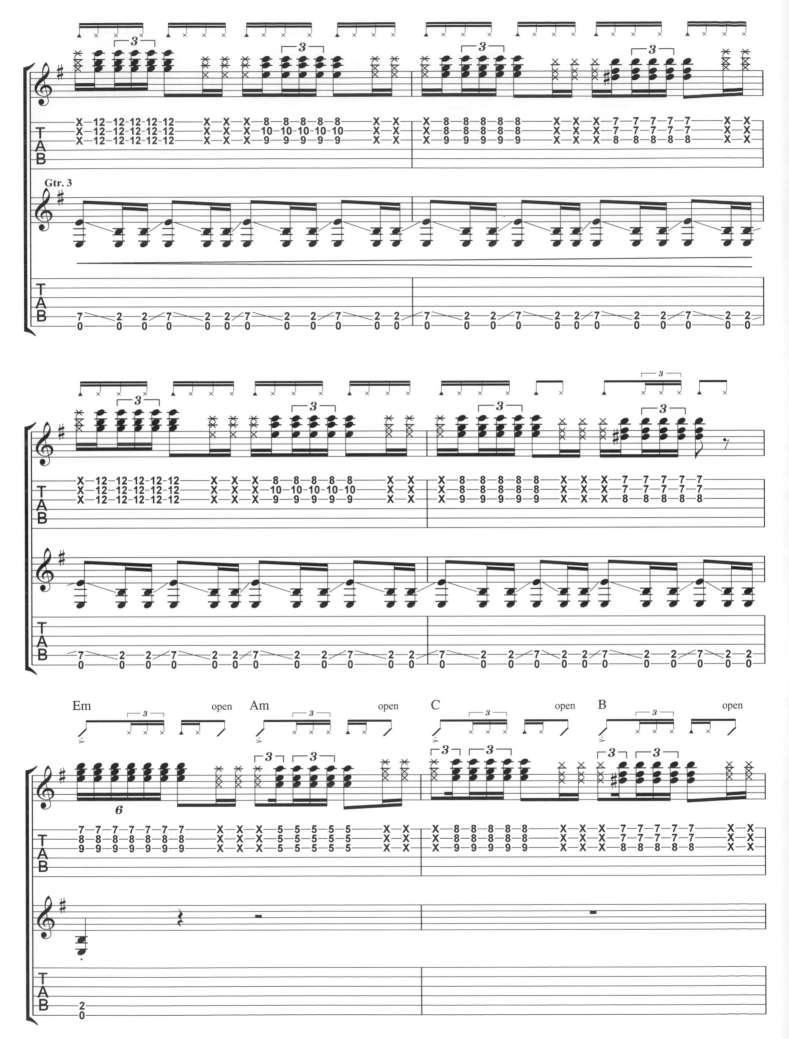

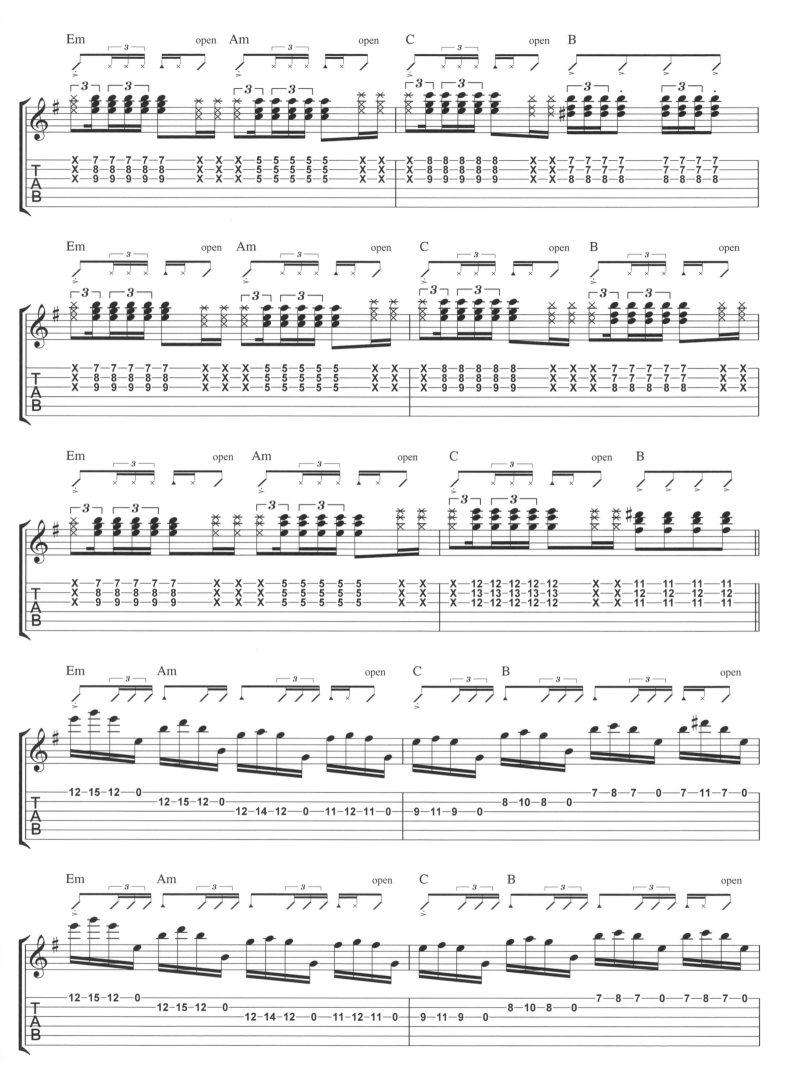

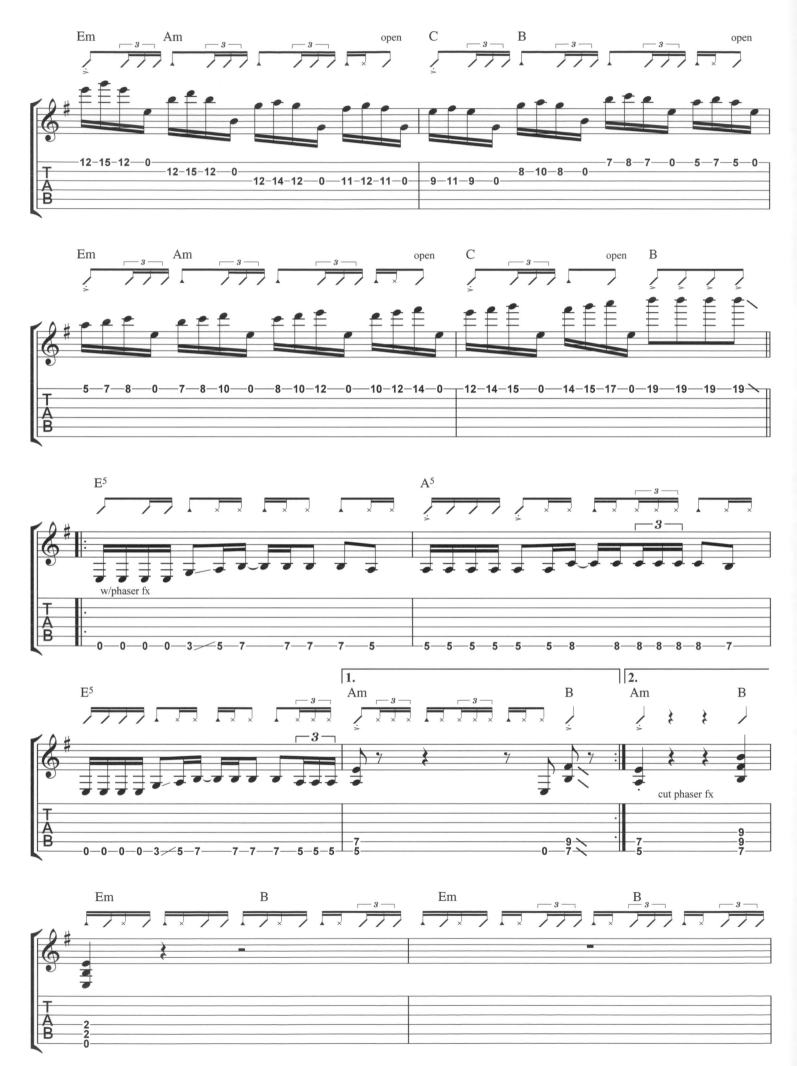

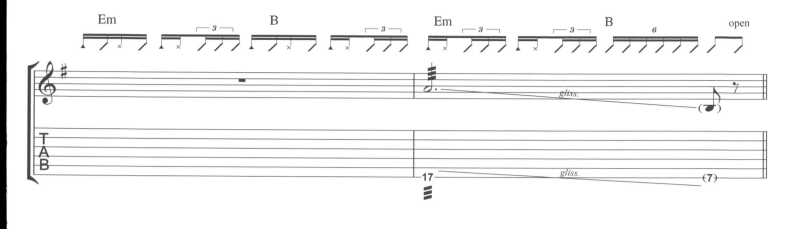

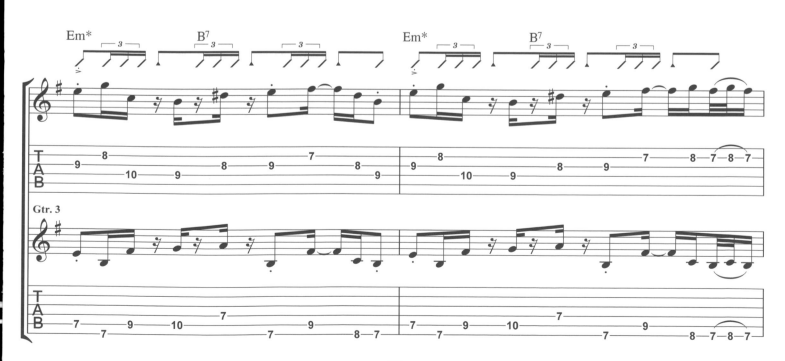

the russian messenger

Music by Rodrigo Sanchez & Gabriela Quintero

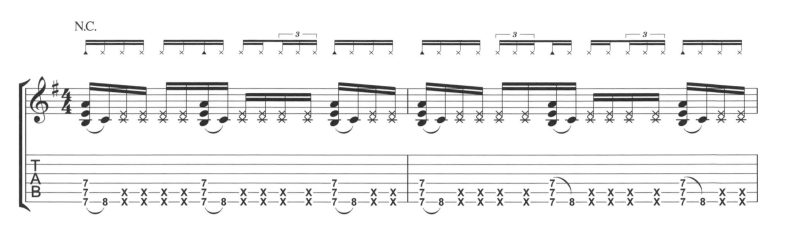

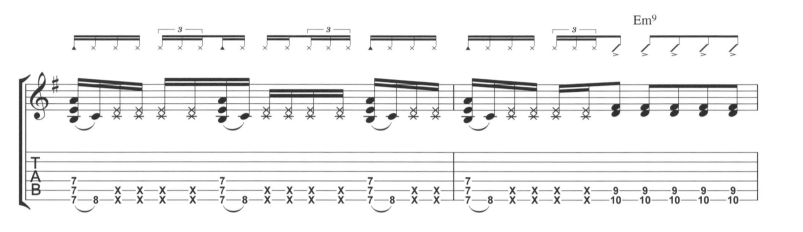

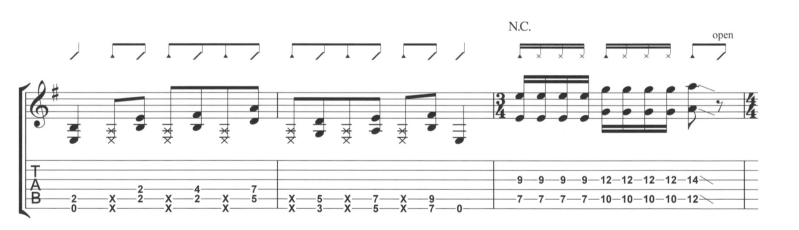

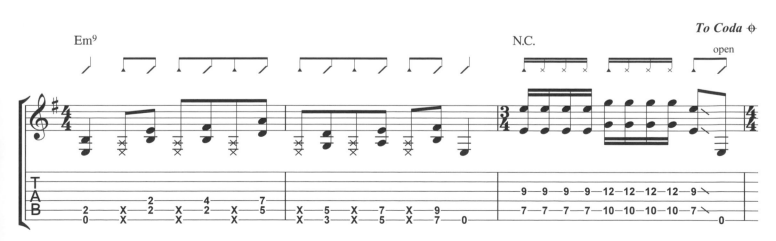

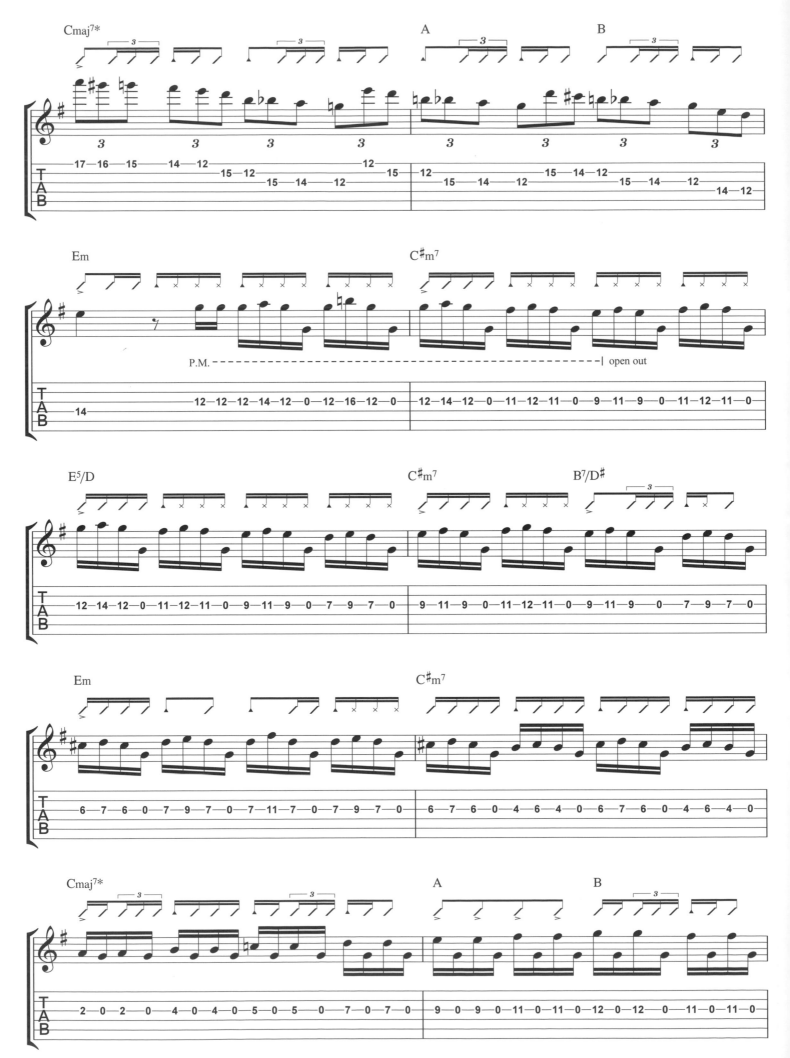

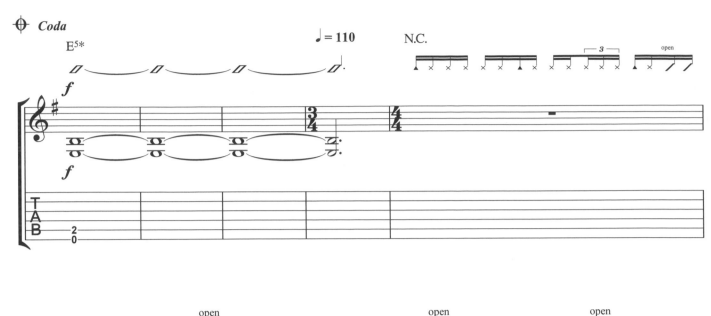

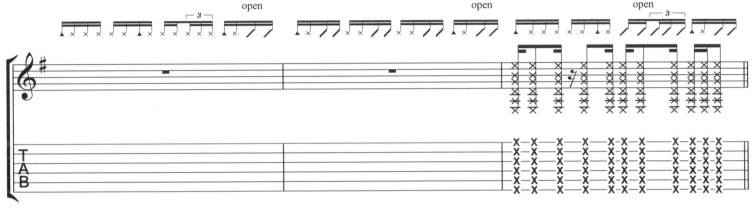

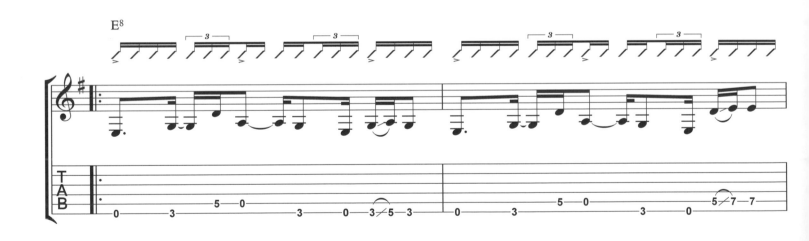

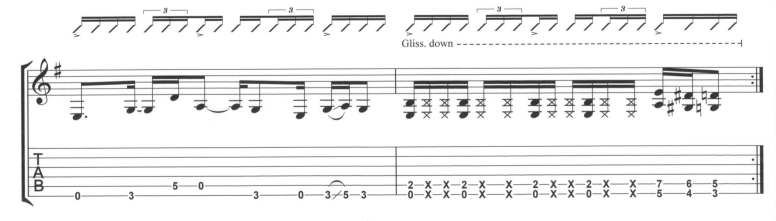

santo domingo

Music by Rodrigo Sanchez & Gabriela Quintero

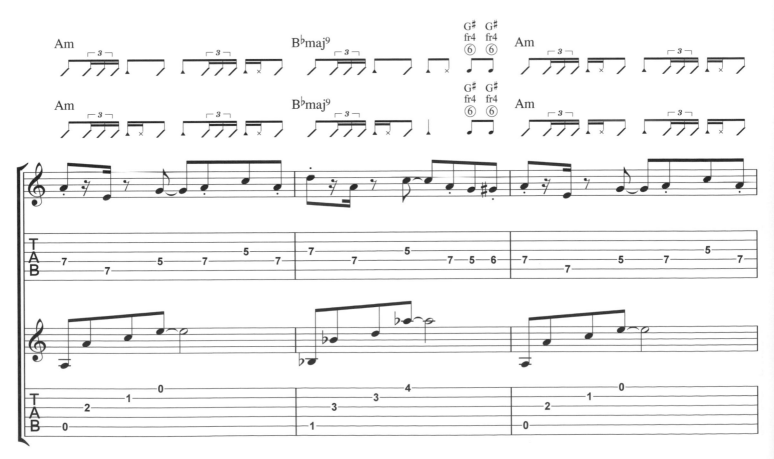

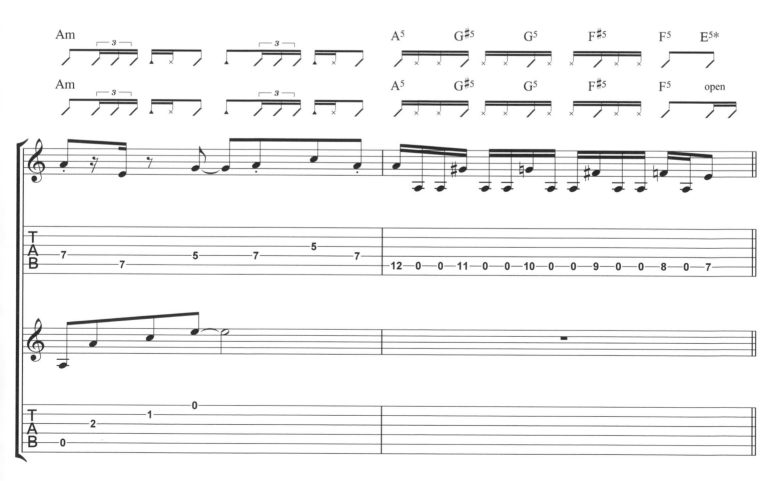

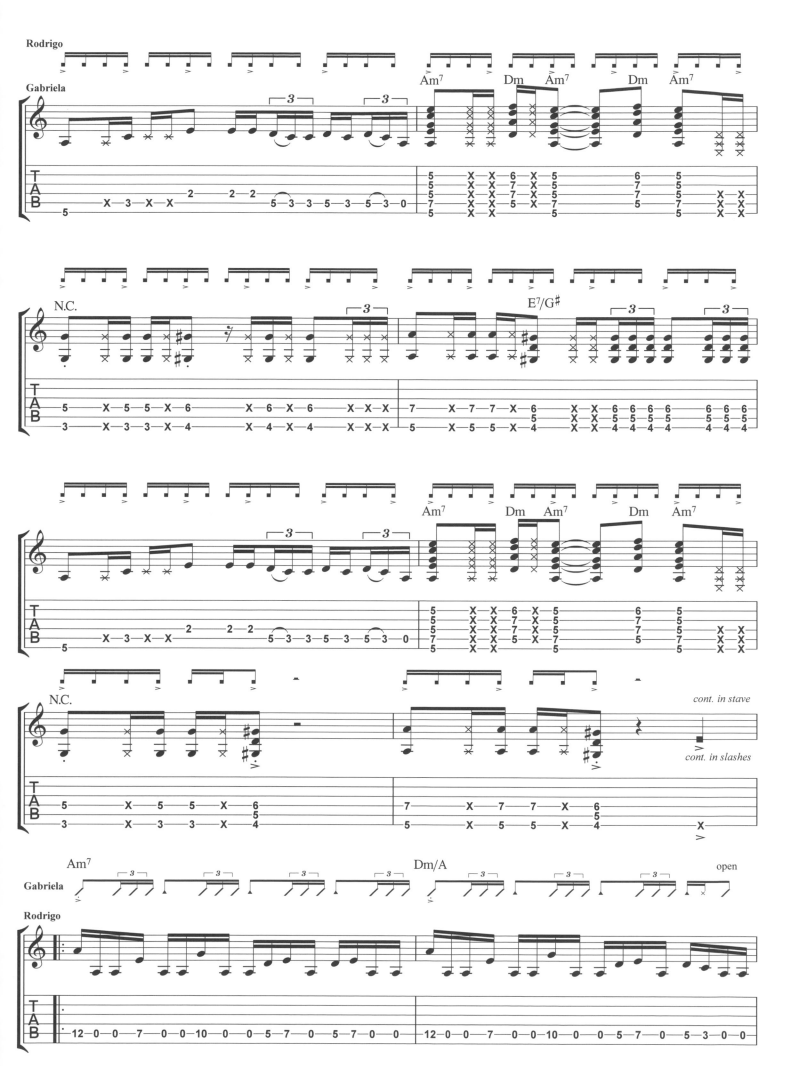

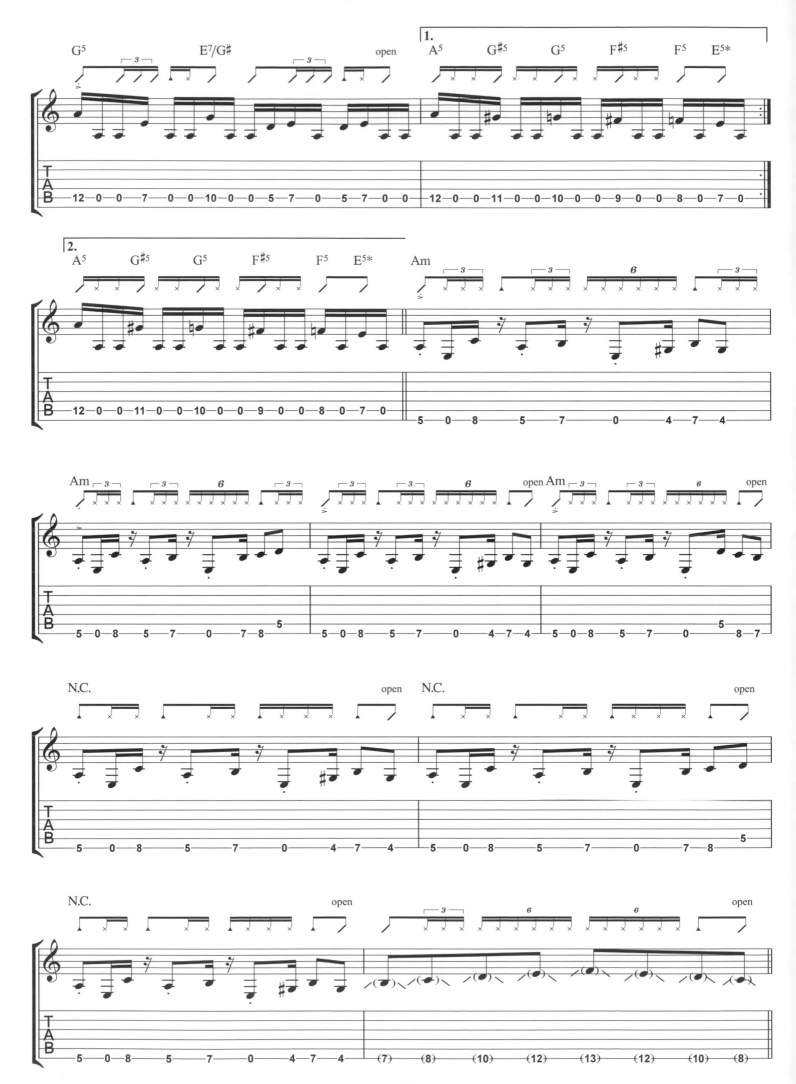

44

the soundmaker

Music by Rodrigo Sanchez & Gabriela Quintero

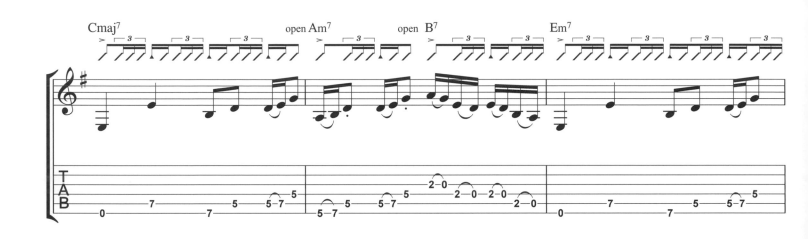

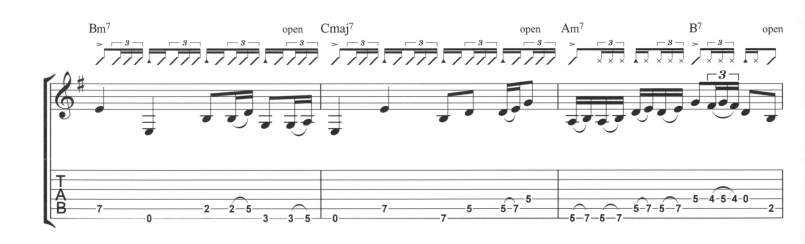

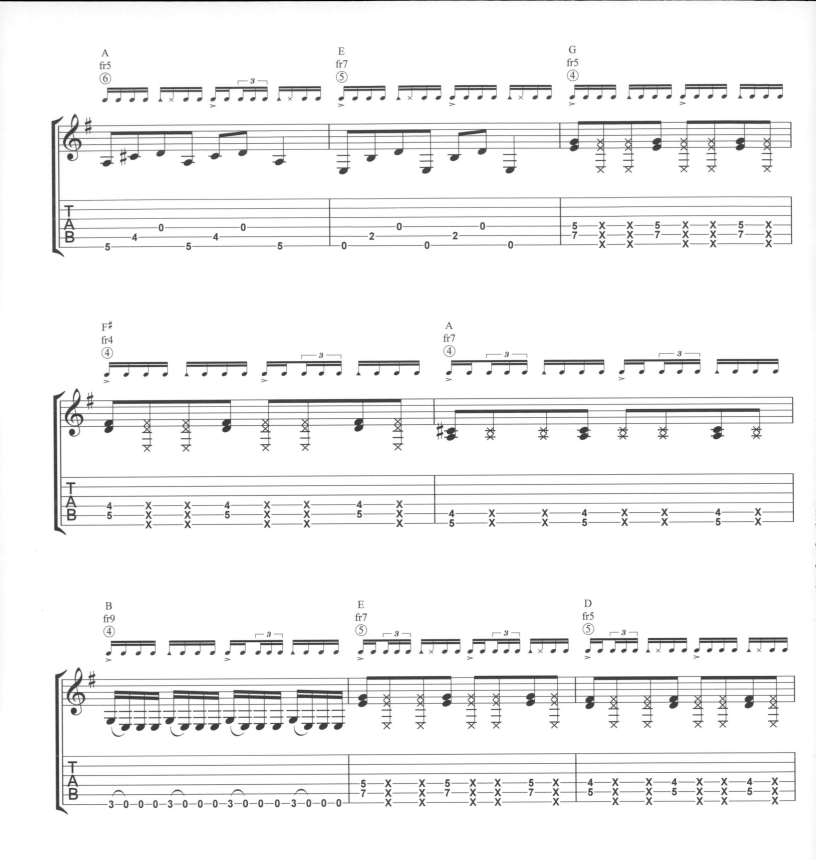
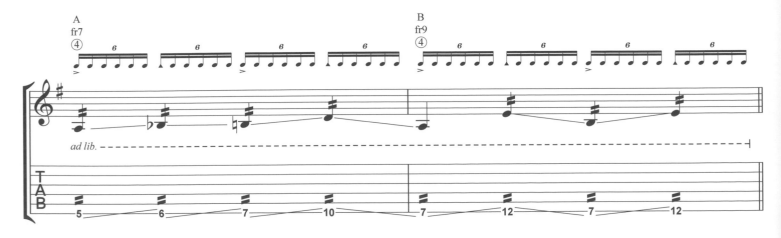

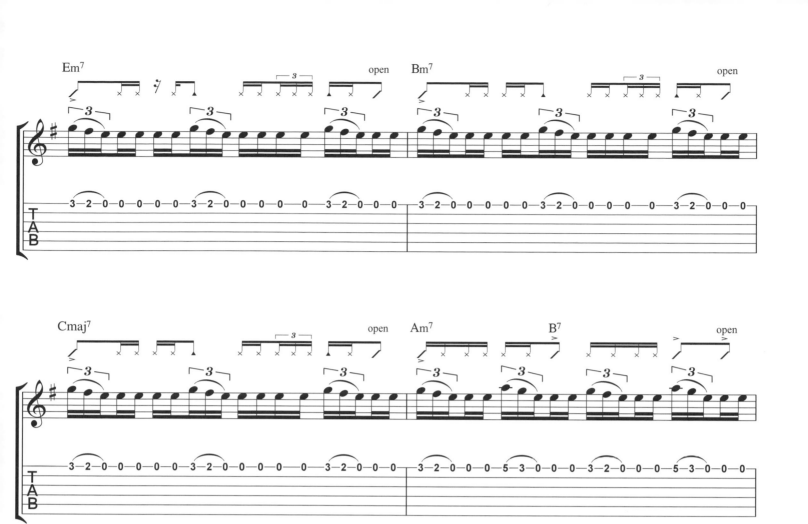

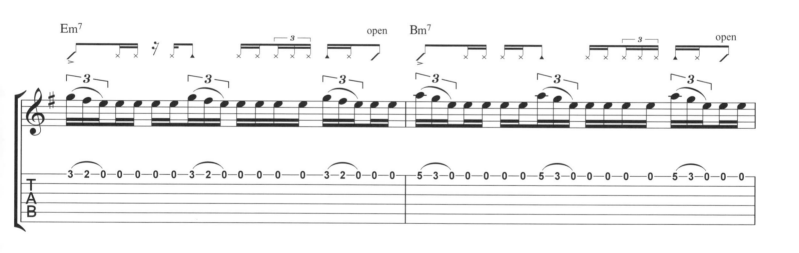

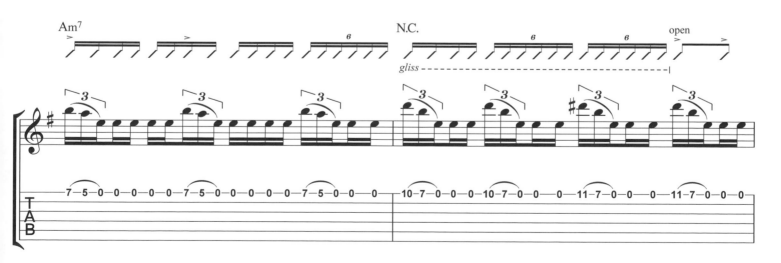

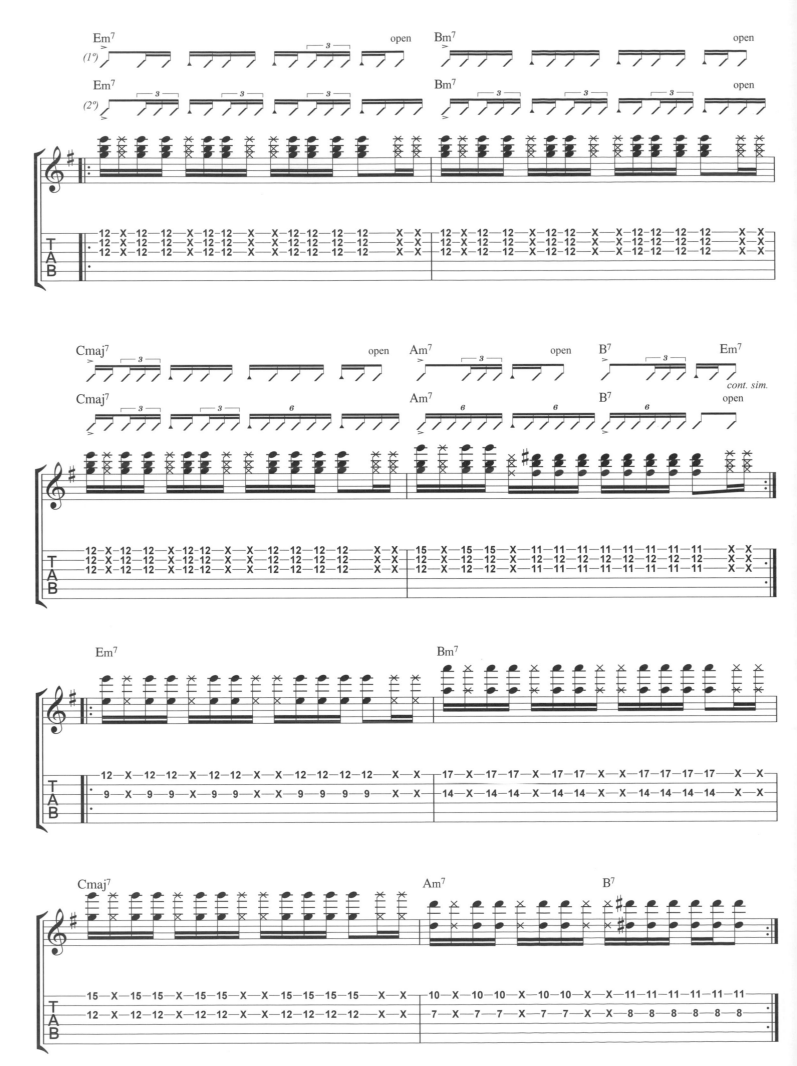

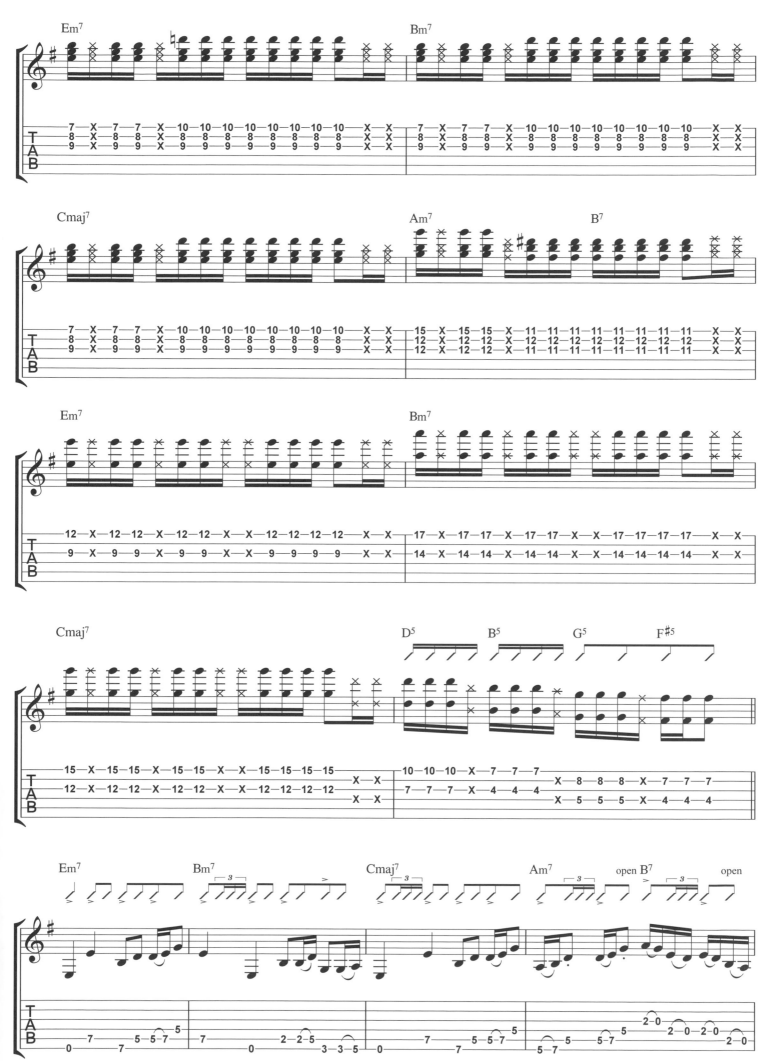

53

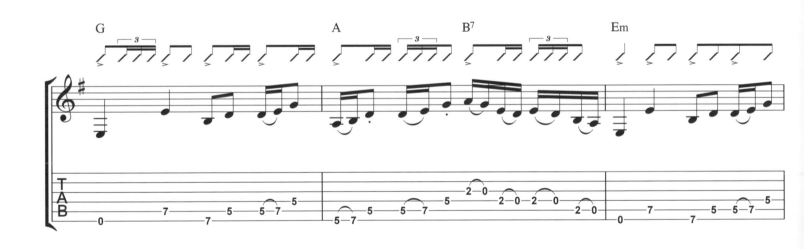

54

tamacun

Music by Rodrigo Sanchez & Gabriela Quintero

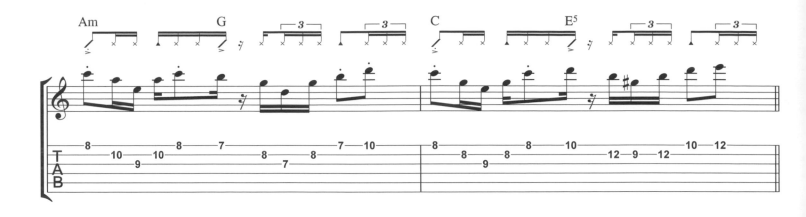

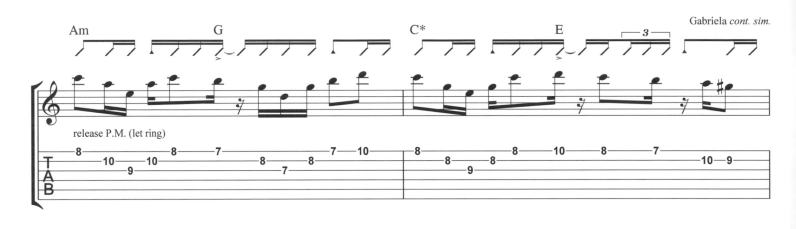

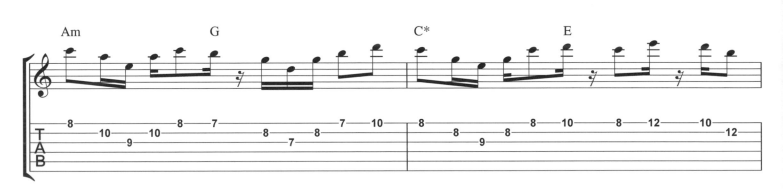

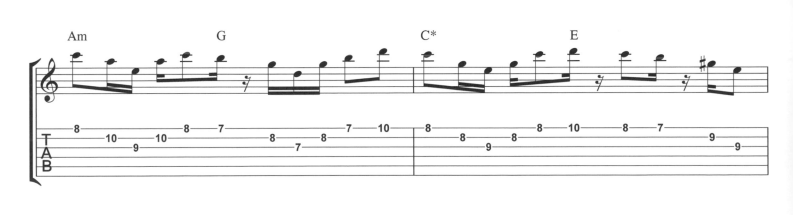

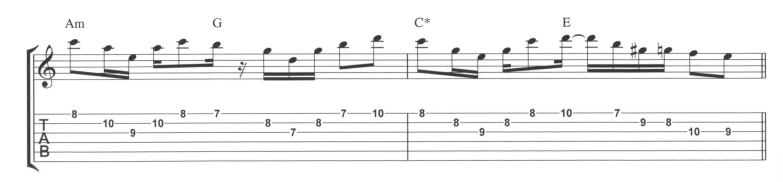

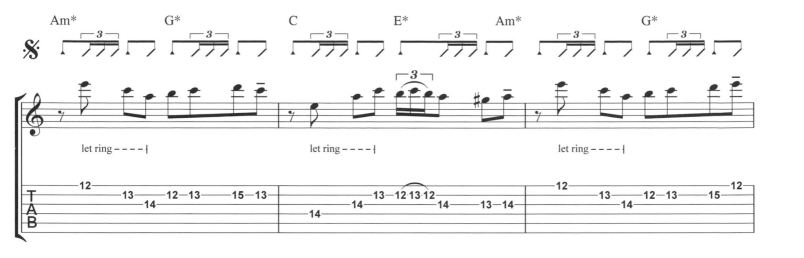

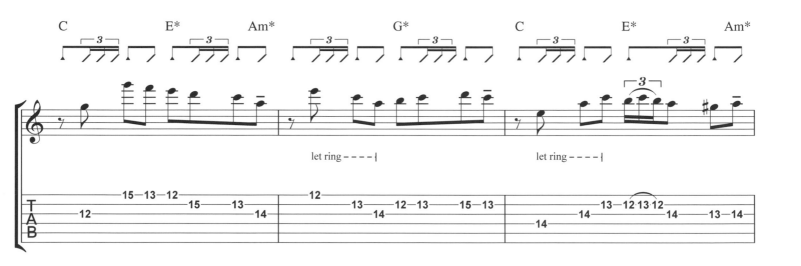

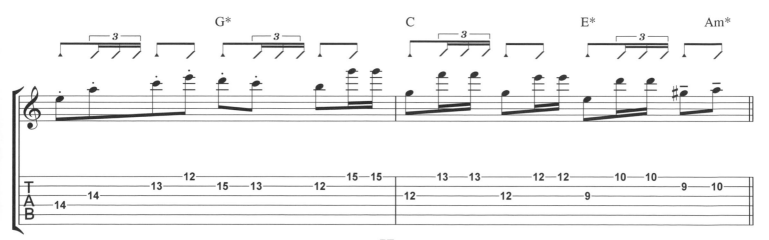

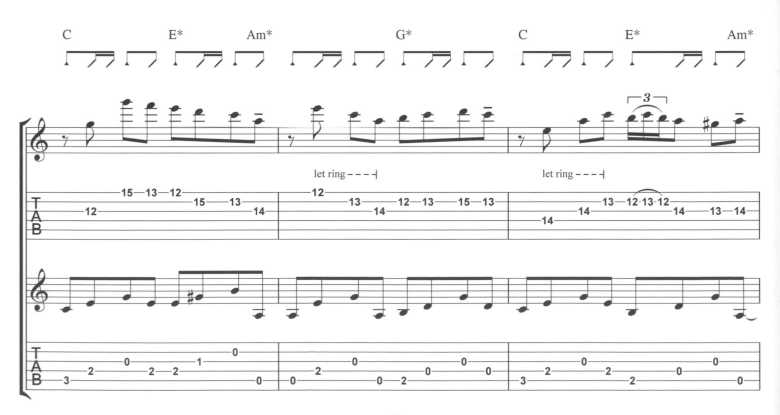

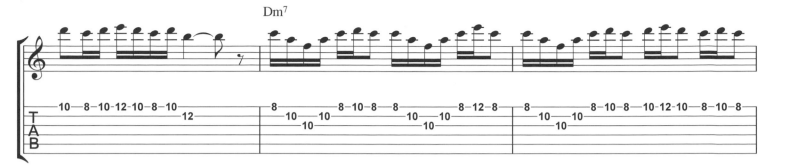

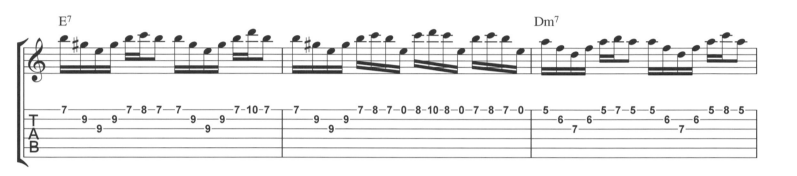

D.S. al Coda

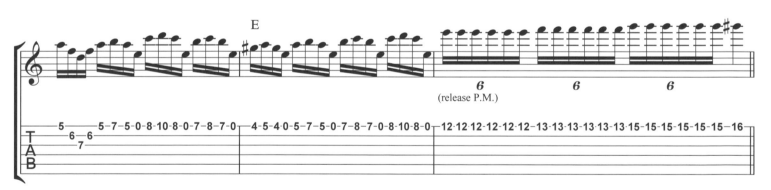

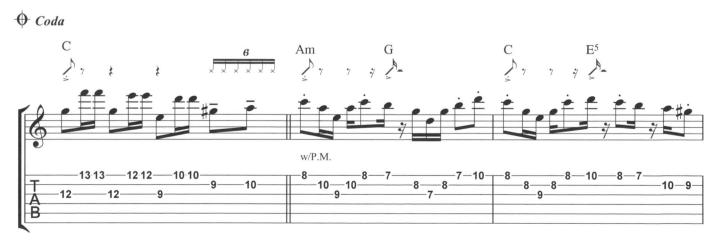

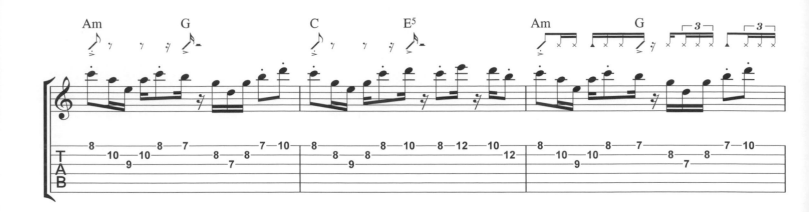

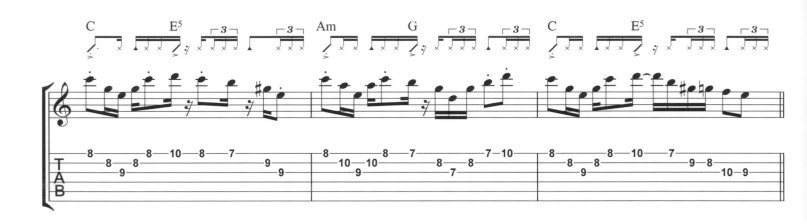

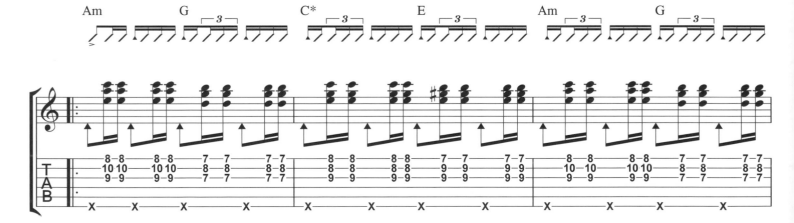

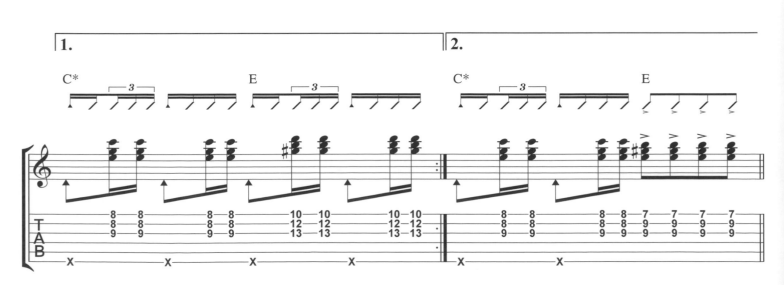

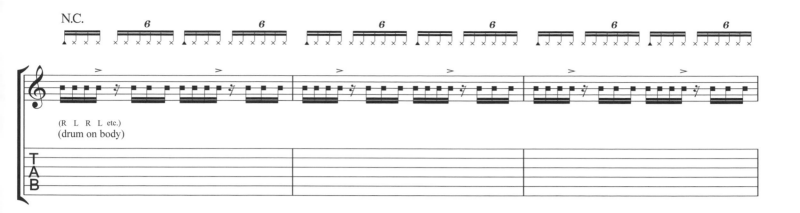

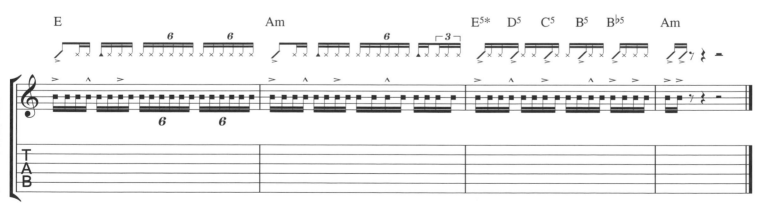

HOW TO DOWNLOAD YOUR MUSIC TRACKS

1. Carefully remove your Download Card from the inside back cover of this book.

2. On the back of the card is your unique access code. Enter this at www.musicsalesdownloads.com

TO REDEEM THIS CARD VISIT
www.musicsalesdownloads.com

ENTER ACCESS CODE:

XXXXXXXXXX

Download Cards are powered by Dropcards.
User must accept terms at dropcards.com/terms
which are adopted by The Music Sales Group.
Not redeemable for cash. Void where prohibited or restricted by law.

DCARD1006478

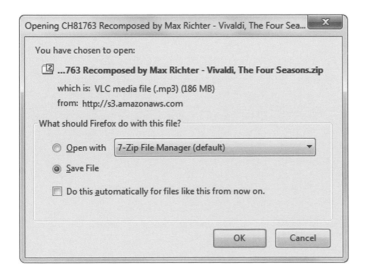

3. Follow the instructions to save your files to your computer*. That's it!

*Appearance of download manager will vary depending upon operating system and web browser.
In case of difficulty when downloading files, please contact dropcards.com/help
Card missing? Please contact music@musicsales.co.uk